River Boy

Contents

OXFORD
UNIVERSITY PRESS

Great Clarendon Street, Oxford OX2 6DP

Oxford University Press is a department of the University of Oxford.
It furthers the University's objective of excellence in research, scholarship,
and education by publishing worldwide in

Oxford   New York

Auckland   Cape Town   Dar es Salaam   Hong Kong   Karachi
Kuala Lumpur   Madrid   Melbourne   Mexico City   Nairobi
New Delhi   Shanghai   Taipei   Toronto

With offices in

Argentina   Austria   Brazil   Chile   Czech Republic   France   Greece
Guatemala   Hungary   Italy   Japan   South Korea   Poland   Portugal
Singapore   Switzerland   Thailand   Turkey   Ukraine   Vietnam

Oxford is a registered trade mark of Oxford University Press
in the UK and in certain other countries

© Frances Gregory 2006

British Library Cataloguing in Publication Data

Data available

ISBN-13: 978-0-19-832655-7

ISBN-10: 0-19-832655-6

10 9 8 7 6 5 4 3 2 1

Printed in Malaysia by Imago.

Acknowledgements

P7 Corel/OUP; **p12tl** Bettmann/Corbis; **p12tr** Adam Woolfitt/
Corbis; **p12b** Bettmann/Corbis.

Illustrations are by Barking Dog Swimmer motif and Annabel Large
pp6, 8, 9, 10/11, 14.

We are grateful for permission to reprint the following copyright mate-
rial in this guide:

Tim Bowler: letter used by permission of the author.

Front cover of Simon Pulse edition of *River Boy* by Tim Bowler used by
permission of Simon & Schuster, Inc and of the artist Rafal Olbinski.

We have tried to trace and contact all copyright holders before publication. If notified, the publisher will be pleased to rectify any errors or
omissions at the earliest opportunity.

Key to icons:

 Pair or group activity

 A resources sheet from the Teacher's
Pack supports this activity.

A Letter from Tim Bowler

Dear Reader

River Boy is a very personal book for me. My grandfather died when I was 14. He was a kindly man and I loved him to bits. When he passed away, I didn't go to his funeral because I was too upset. Later I regretted this and though it would be wrong to say I've been haunted by it ever since, I believe one subconscious reason for writing *River Boy* was to say goodbye to my grandfather, to 'go to his funeral' so to speak, through the experiences of my fictional characters, and to tell him once again how much I loved and still love him.

The other reason for writing *River Boy*, of course, was to tell a story. I didn't want myself or my grandfather to appear in recognizable form. So the main character is not a boy of 14 but a girl of 15, and the grandfather is not a calm, serene man but a crusty, awkward one. To begin with I just sat down at my computer and started typing out possible ingredients.

The first two were my main characters: young girl, tetchy grandfather. At this point my wife stuck her head round the door and asked me how I was getting on, and did I have a title yet? The moment she asked about the title, I heard myself say: 'River Boy'. To this day I don't know where that came from. But it felt right and suddenly I had four ingredients: girl, grandfather, river, boy.

Then a few days later, my wife came home with a painting she'd bought. It was a river scene. No people in it and no title, just a mysterious river. We hung it on the wall and suddenly I realized that the grandfather in my story is an artist, that he's painting a river picture, a picture with no people, a picture called River Boy. And so the novel began. I didn't know at first that the river was going to become a spiritual metaphor and that the story was going to take me on a journey too, just like Jess. But I'm glad I made that journey. I'm glad I wrote *River Boy*. I'm glad I said goodbye.

Tim Bowler

How Good are First Impressions?

What's in a name?

What does a title like *River Boy* suggest the novel will be about? Who will be the main character? What themes will be tackled? Will it be an adventure story? A mystery story? A detective story? Fantasy or science fiction?

Judging a book by its cover

Just the title isn't much to go on, is it? You can have a good but rather general guess about the content. The cover might tell us more, though.

What can you tell about *River Boy* from the cover on your copy of the novel?

- ◉ What can you predict about the plot?
- ◉ What characters might be involved?
- ◉ Where will the events take place?
- ◉ Will this be a serious or a comic book?
- ◉ Write down those ideas, so you can check how right you were later on.

Try some other covers too!

During its life a book doesn't have just one cover. Look at these other covers *River Boy* has had.

- ◉ What similarities and differences can you spot in the cover designs? Do they help you to predict anything?

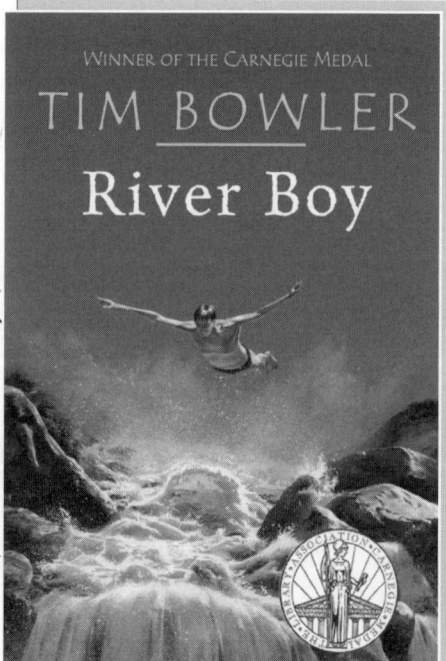

River Boy

Reading the blurb

These words appear on one of these front covers. What do they suggest about the story you are about to read?

The boy was part of the mystery of this place. Perhaps the whole mystery.

- ⊙ Who is this boy? What place? What mystery?
- ⊙ Are any of the ideas you first had about the title beginning to change?

These words make up the blurb on the back cover:

It didn't start with the river boy. It started, as so many things started, with Grandpa, and with swimming. It was only later, when she came to think things over, that she realized that in a strange way the river boy had been part of her all along, like the figment of a dream.
And the dream was her life.

- ⊙ What questions would you like to ask about this bit of text?
- ⊙ What firm predictions can you now make about the story that you will read?

Opening words

The words quoted here are also the opening words of the novel. Now that you know how the story begins, does it change your questions or your predictions?

Did you expect the story to begin with these words?

One question, one prediction

Before you begin reading *River Boy*, decide on your most **important question** about the novel, and your most **certain prediction**.

Now, you're ready to begin reading. As you turn the pages, see how accurately you've predicted, and whether you can find the answers to those questions.

River Boy

Exploring a New Place

 *Holiday destination?*

TO LET

CHARMING HOLIDAY COTTAGE TO LET

Braymouth 45 miles. In the beautiful Braybourne Valley. Secluded cottage. Perfect for active family, keen on sport and swimming, fishing, and hill walking. Unspoilt countryside. Magnificent views of rugged hills. River Bray runs close by the cottage. Delightful sound of running water as river makes its way through this fertile valley.

Accommodation sleeps 4/5. Generous sitting room, kitchen and small cloakroom on ground floor. A large downstairs games room can be used as a bedroom. Two further bedrooms and modern bathroom upstairs. Well maintained and cared for by local family.

£365 per calendar week in season.
For further details contact ngray@btinternet.org or phone 01232 897654

What's your view?

⊙   What might be the appeal of this place as a holiday destination?
⊙   Which words or phrases in the advertisement are designed to persuade possible visitors?

Judging by the pictures

What words can you add to describe this place, to add to the detail given in the advertisement? Start with the cottage, then move on to the scenery. Share a few of your ideas with your class.

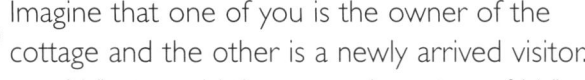

Place

Let's go there

What would it be like to stay at this holiday cottage?

Imagine that one of you is the owner of the cottage and the other is a newly arrived visitor.

- What would the owner have to say? What questions might the visitor ask? Use the pictures on these pages to give you ideas.

- The owner can take the visitor on an imaginary guided tour, telling the visitor about the lovely natural surroundings – the river, the hills, the country lanes. To make the imagination work really well, the visitor can close his or her eyes.

- Visitors, share with the whole class some of the sensations that have been described to you. What are the best things about this place?

Role reversal

Next, swap roles. This time the owner can put in more detail, building on all the shared ideas about how this place will appeal to each of the senses. How does it feel to be here?

Share your impressions with your class – you could make a list of the most popular words used by everyone in their descriptions.

Top Tip

Remember... your words should help to persuade others to visit the cottage and its rural location.

Satisfied customers

Compose a satisfied holidaymaker's comment that could be used in the holiday brochure. Write your comments on a card to add to the display. You might write 'Fresh air, unspoilt landscape, sparkling river water!' or 'Our rural retreat – stunning river views'.

Quick Quiz

Read on to the end of Chapter 2 in *River Boy*:

1 What does Jess think of their holiday cottage?

2 Why did Grandpa want to come back to a deserted place like this?

A Family Story

What do we know so far?

So what do we know about the characters from *River Boy* that we have met so far? How do they feel about each other?

 Use the pictures and quotations from *River Boy* to help you think…

'You seem to be a sort of muse for him… after you were born, it's like something started to motivate him, and it's gone on motivating him ever since… there's something… he gets from you, something really important to him.'
(Mum to Jess, pages 10–11)

She helped him and took his hand. It seemed so withered now, not like it used to be. Again she thought back to the days when she had been little and his hands had held her and made her feel safe. Now those hands were taking strength from hers.
(Jess of Grandpa, page 20)

An only son… the two… constantly at loggerheads… such different men, one fiercely independent, fiercely driven; the other mild and unambitious.
(Jess on Dad and Grandpa, page 5)

'Everything changes, Jess. Everything. Nothing stays the same. Nothing lasts forever.'
(Grandpa to Jess, page 21)

'Jess, give your Dad plenty of support. I know you will anyway but, remember, if it's hard for you, it's worse for him. OK?'
(Mum to Jess, page 5)

It was hard to think of Grandpa dying… She didn't want to think of change. She wanted to think of everything being the same forever.
(Jess on Grandpa, pages 19 and 21)

Hopes and fears

- What **most** worries each of the characters at the beginning of the novel?
- What does each most want or need to achieve at this point in his or her life?

Characters in the background

Why does Tim Bowler take the family on a holiday to such an isolated, remote place? Jess enjoys her own company – she's like Grandpa in that – but wouldn't she prefer friends her own age?

Then there's Alfred – Grandpa mentions him at the end of Chapter 2.

'Do you think you'll remember the place?' she said.
''Course I will. I was born there.'
'But you were fifteen when you left.'
'That's right. Same age as you.'
(Grandpa and Jess, page 7)

The waters slipped past, dark and sleek, gurgling over the rocks just down from her window… part of her seemed to run with them, all the way to the sea.
(page 19)

'Alfred… used to live round here when I was a boy. Same age as me. His folks had a cottage about two miles from here… Can't imagine Alfred'd be any different… if he's still… alive…'
(page 21)

Mystery hero

◉ Who's the hero in this story? Jess? Grandpa? What about the novel's title? Is that the missing boy in Grandpa's painting? Or is there someone or something else?

Remember what Jess feels after she swims in the river for the first time:

'The feeling started to grow that she had not been – and was not – alone.' (page 26)

Linking Jess, Grandpa and the river

Remember how Tim Bowler describes the river?

> It was as though there were a spirit here… a spirit of the river…a spirit running through all this like a magic charm. (page 19)

Finally, discuss what Tim Bowler says (www.timbowler.co.uk) about remote places:

> *I love isolated places. I love wild places, places with a powerful atmosphere. A location is like another character in the story. It has its own personality and that personality impacts on the story just as the characters do. Isolated locations are particularly evocative because they place the characters in isolation, too, where they are often at their most vulnerable. Some people thrive in lonely spots, others fall to pieces. Isolation can bring out fear and it can bring out courage.*

Keep these thoughts in mind as you read on …

River Boy

Grandpa's Painting: 'River Boy'

Grandpa's Pa

He was so obsessive about a painting once he had started it, and this one –
this one she sensed was important to him. And, for some reason, also to her.
(pages 11–12)

Why so important?

- ⦿ Why is the painting important to Grandpa?
- ⦿ Why should it be important for Jess?

Here are some of things we are told about the picture. Can you imagine it?

> An unframed painting, unmistakably one of Grandpa's yet unlike anything he had done before; and clearly nowhere near finished… There was a river, which dominated the scene, not a river she recognized and perhaps not even a real one at all, just a fantasy river. The picture was strange and amorphous… eerily beautiful. The banks were a subtle hint of green that the eye barely took in, being somehow drawn into the pale waters and away towards a hidden sea. There were no animals, no birds, no people; and it felt right that way. There seemed no place for living things in this remote vision. Yet for some reason she found herself thinking of the coming of autumn, after a long, rich summer.
>
> *(pages 8–9)*

> And the image that haunted her most was that of the boy, the river boy; the boy who wasn't there.
>
> *(page 28)*

> The more she looked at it, the more the presence of the absent boy seemed to grow, until finally it overwhelmed everything, the banks and the sky and even the river itself, pulling her into the picture and onwards, irresistibly, towards the sea.
>
> *(page 12)*

> He had to finish the picture… he needed a brush to shape the visions of his inner life.
>
> *(page 28)*

River Boy

She saw images of a boy who appeared where there should be no boy; and images of a painting where a boy should be but was not; and she saw Grandpa, the thread upon which this paradox seemed to hang.
(page 71)

He had added so much more. The hints of green that had suggested the river banks were darker and had touches of brown; the pale waters had flecks of silver and gold and blue; but the picture was now dominated by swirls of mist and a strange tension in the water as it was drawn down a widening mouth towards the sea. There was still a remoteness about the scene, yet it seemed more haunting, more disturbing than ever.
And still there was no boy.
(page 33)

'If he can just finish the thing, maybe he'll get some peace of mind.'
(Mum, page 64)

Every painting he'd ever started had been an obsession with him until he'd managed to tear it out of himself, and now this unfulfilled part of his soul would rot away inside him, colouring the last hours of his life.
(pages 85–86)

'He's trying to paint a picture. It's an important picture. It really matters to him and he can't finish it. His hands and arms are too weak.'
(Jess, page 89)

'You finish the picture...
you be his hands.'
(The river boy, page 89)

Will Grandpa finish the painting?
Will he paint in the boy that Jess expects? Will she recognize him?

River Boy

Jess – Champion Swimmer

All she needed now… was a big swimming challenge; something to test herself against. (page 2)

Do you know…?

What do you know about long-distance swimming? What about swimming across the English Channel?

Do you know who the first people to swim the English Channel were?

These articles will help you find out more.

The First Man to Swim the English Channel

Born in Shropshire in 1848, Matthew Webb learned to swim in the River Severn.

On 24 August 1875, smeared in porpoise oil, Webb dived into the water near Dover's Admiralty Pier. Twenty-one hours and 45 minutes later he waded ashore at Calais, much to the delight of the passengers and crew of the mailship *The Maid of Kent*, who witnessed his final efforts.

Webb died in 1883 when he hit his

Webb learned to swim up river from Ironbridge in Shropshire, where he saved his younger brother Thomas from drowning in the summer of 1863

head on jagged rocks in a whirlpool at the foot of Niagara Falls. He had hoped to earn a fortune of £12,000 by swimming under and across the swirling water.

The First Woman Channel Swimmer

In August 1926, New Yorker Gertrude Ederle, aged 20, swam from Cape Griz-Nez in France to Kingsdown in England. Despite stormy weather, her time of 14 hours 30 minutes beat the men's record by more than two hours.

'People said women couldn't swim the Channel. I proved they could,' said Ederle, in an interview marking the 75th anniversary of her feat.

She died in 2004, at the age of 98, after a life dedicated to endurance swimming.

Repeating the challenge?

British-born Alison Streeter has swum the English Channel no less than 43 times (and that's only up to 2005), and she has also swum the notorious 18-mile stretch of water between Ireland and Scotland in record time.

Swimming for Someone You Love

Jane McCormick, 23, prepared to swim the English Channel by training in the Manchester Ship Canal. Her swim from Dover to Calais in July 2005 was in a good cause – to raise money for Headway, a charity for survivors of brain injury.

Jane's brother suffered brain damage in a street attack. 'Sean, our other brother Dominic and I used to swim in a club together, so this seemed like the logical thing to do,' she said.

A student of fashion at Manchester Metropolitan University, Jane planned the swim to coincide with the warming of the water to about 16°C.

Jess's big challenge

How will Jess's challenge compare with these swimmers'? Will she reach the river boy before he swims out to sea?

Read Chapter 18 in *River Boy* to find out...

Job at the BBC?

You've nearly landed a job at the BBC News website. To pass the final test, you're sent to interview Jess (and those who know her) about the swim to Braymouth.

The editor has given you the challenge of writing a 250-word article with one good photo all about Jess's achievement. The article on Jane McCormick above is your model. The editor wants you to include:

⊙ all the facts (who, what, where, why and when)
⊙ some words from someone who was there.

So get your interview questions ready. You've got to be back with the article finished by the afternoon.

Take turns with a partner to plan the role of the would-be journalist and the person being interviewed.

Ending the Journey

Cover comments

Do you remember how the opening words of the novel were printed on the back of *River Boy*?

> *It didn't start with the river boy. It started, as so many things started, with Grandpa, and with swimming...*

Would a comment from the publisher or a reviewer have been better? What about this one?

> *Grandpa is dying. He can barely move his hands any more but, stubborn as ever, refuses to stay in hospital. He's determined to finish his last painting, 'River Boy', before he goes.*
> *At first Jess can't understand his refusal to let go, but then she too becomes involved in the mysterious painting. And when she meets the river boy himself, she finds she is suddenly caught up in a challenge of her own that she must complete – before it's too late...*

Accept the challenge

See if you can write an alternative 'blurb'. The example above has about 80 words. Your publisher demands 50 words only, and you have five minutes to compose it, so get a move on!

How did you get on? Now read on...

River Boy

Reviewing the reviews

Below are some of the first opinions published about *River Boy*. Do you agree or disagree with each of these comments?

'A river is a natural metaphor for life and death and Tim Bowler uses it to wonderful effect in this lovely simple story. *River Boy* is written in quiet, non-poetic prose – but it's a poem, as well as a very moving novel.'
Susan Cooper

'It's an intense, mystic exploration of the relationship between a teenage girl and her irascible grandfather, an artist. Bowler's writing creates indelible visual images.'
Time Out

'Beautifully written... it feels like a written painting, a descriptive, emotive work that will mean something different to each reader. This mystical story is a true work of literature.'
Voya

'The atmosphere is haunting, the sense of the power beyond ourselves, strong and silent, and the mystery of the natural world, woodlands and airy hills and sliding, glittering water are beautifully suggested, as is the strength – oh, subject most rare – of familial love.'
The Spectator

'*River Boy* has all the hallmarks of a classic – it deepens with re-reading, and takes the reader on a journey. You are not the same person at the end of this book.'
Carnegie Medal judges

'*River Boy* is strong on mood and atmosphere. It deals with death unpretentiously and unsentimentally, investigating the final stages with dignity and calm.'
The Guardian

'Unflinchingly facing down the subject of death, Bowler elevates it into an elegiac, magical depiction of a granddaughter's relationship with her grandfather.'
Scotland on Sunday

'A lyrical story of bereavement that manages not to be effete thanks to credible and courageous characters and a plot that involves mystery and tension.'
The Sunday Times

Find your own reviews

Several book websites encourage readers to send in their opinions – positive and negative! Take a look at some of these websites for yourself – just type 'River Boy' and 'Tim Bowler' into a search engine to find them.

 ## Your journey

Describe the journey that *River Boy* took you on.
- ⦿ Where did you begin?
- ⦿ What did you notice on the way?
- ⦿ How did your emotions change as you moved through the story?
- ⦿ Where did you end up and how do you feel?
- ⦿ Now listen to your partner's description of his or her journey.

River Boy

Pathways... to Another Good Read

Here are some ideas for books to compare with *River Boy*.

Contemporary texts

For other books by Tim Bowler – look at
www.timbowler.co.uk

Ruby Holler by Sharon Creech
ISBN 0-7475-6029-3

For as long as they can remember, Dallas and Florida have lived in the Trepids' orphanage. Many families have tried to foster them but the brother and sister have earned the name of the 'Trouble Twins'. Not until Sairy and Tiller come along does anyone have any success. They seem the perfect couple to adopt the 'Trouble Twins'.

Goodnight Mr Tom by Michelle Magorian
ISBN 0-1413-0144-9

During the Second World War, eight-year-old evacuee Willie Beech is suddenly transferred from a deprived London background into the heart of the country. Dumped on grumpy old Tom Oakley, the sharp-tongued widower, Willie soon finds that Mister Tom is fair and friendly.

The Edge by Alan Gibbons
ISBN 0752861409

'We've got to go. Now.' Danny and his mother must escape from Chris, his mother's boyfriend, a violent man who beats them both up, and won't let them go. Traveling north and taking refuge with Danny's grandparents they hope they are safe, but Chris eventually tracks them down. Danny must learn to confront his worst fears.

Tell the Moon To Come Out by Joan Lingard
ISBN 0-1413-1689-6

It's 1939, and Spain is a country torn apart by civil war. Nick has come from Scotland in search of his father – who left the family home three years ago to fight in Spain. He never came back.

Memory by Margaret Mahy
ISBN 0-0071-2337-X

It's the fifth anniversary of his sister's death, and 19-year-old Jonny Dart is still troubled by guilt and a confused memory of the accident that took her life. He goes in search of the only other witness to the fatal event – his sister's best friend. He finds the answers he needs from an unlikely character: Sophie, an old woman with Alzheimer's.

Pre-1914 texts

Our Mutual Friend by Charles Dickens
ISBN 0-1928-3523-8

The river is a villain in *Our Mutual Friend*. The river is an enemy to truth. It swallows up stories as easily as it swallows up the bodies of the drowned.

Silas Marner by George Eliot
ISBN 0-1928-3458-4

Falsely accused, cut off from his past, Silas the weaver is reduced to a spider-like existence, endlessly weaving his web and hoarding his gold. Meanwhile Godfrey Cass, son of the squire, contracts a secret marriage. While the village celebrates Christmas and New Year, Silas's hoards of gold are stolen and miraculously replaced by a small child with golden curls.

River Boy